Vincent

PARK
LANE

"The French air clears the brain and does one good – a world of good."

Vincent van Gogh

"To express the love of two lovers through a marriage of two complementary colours, their mingling and their opposition, the mysterious vibrations of kindred tones. To express the thought of a brow by the radiance of a light tone against a dark background. To express hope by a handful of stars..."

That was 33-year old Vincent van Gogh, writing from Provence in 1888 to his brother Theo, describing what he was trying to achieve in his paintings. By that time, painting had become the all-consuming passion that gave meaning to Vincent's life. But it had not always been so. Before turning to painting, this difficult and idealistic Dutchman, the eldest of five children of a Protestant minister, had known other passions.

Born on March 30th, 1853 in Zundert, a small village in Brabant, Holland, where his father was a minister, Vincent was a dreamy and shy boy. Sensitive and close to his family, Vincent loved to take long solitary walks along the flat fields of the Dutch countryside, studying the plants and insects he came across. The only person whose company he enjoyed on these walks was his brother Theo, four years younger than he. Theirs was to be a close relationship that would last throughout their lives.

Vincent left his formal studies early. His family was large and as the eldest, he had to earn a living. Although he was unsure of what he wanted to do in life, an uncle in Paris offered him a job in The Hague that seemed too good to miss. It was a modest start, consisting of wrapping and mailing books, but it was in a prestigious art gallery, a branch of the Galerie Goupil in Paris. In The Hague, Vincent, who was now sixteen, first revealed what came to be one of his most characteristic qualities, a capacity to take in what was happening all around him. As he wrapped and unwrapped packages, he listened to conversations about art and literature, saw paintings, looked at engravings and fed the curiosity that his reading and visits to museums were awakening. Indeed, his own family was not uninterested in culture. Vincent's mother, Anne Cornélie Barbentus, the daughter of a bookbinder, also loved to read, far more than her husband, and she showed some skill at drawing as well. Among the family ancestors there had been jewellers and at least one sculptor.

In 1873 Vincent was transferred to the London branch of the Galerie Goupil. Though not a promotion, it was a move he made willingly, for his vagabond spirit saw it as a chance to explore a new place. Reading Dickens had given him certain ideas about London and when he got there, he loved to take long walks through the streets, meeting

The Sower, 1890

a kind of people he had never before seen or imagined. Yet, as he explored the poorest and most miserable neighbourhoods of the city, he was still the same curious and dreamy young man who had walked the fields of Brabant.

By now Vincent was no longer an adolescent. In London, he fell hopelessly in love with his handlady's daughter, Eugenie. But the object of his dreams quickly became the cause of his unhappiness. She was secretly engaged to another man, and when Vincent declared his feelings to her, she rejected him, laughing. His heart bruised, he decided to sublimate his suffering in religion and to spend his life working to help others. Soon after, he was transferred to Paris.

By 1875, installed at the head branch of the famous Galerie Goupil, Vincent should have felt proud and happy. In fact, although Paris helped him develop his interest in art, it did nothing to resolve his spiritual crisis, as existential as it was sentimental. He visited exhibitions and museums but more often than not he shut himself up in his room with a friend to read and study the Bible. Religion and a religious vocation were at the centre of his thoughts; noble obsessions tormented him. He began to neglect his work so much that he was finally asked to resign. No one could persuade him to give up his interest in religion, not even his brother Theo, who usually had some influence over him. Theo had been encouraging Vincent to dedicate himself to painting, which he felt was Vincent's true vocation, not saving souls.

Although they were separated by long distances, Theo kept up an affectionate contact with Vincent. The two brothers wrote regularly, visited each other, and spent Christmases together at the family home in one or another of the villages where their father preached his sermons. Often in the letters he sent to his brother, Vincent drew little sketches describing places he had seen and people he had met. Vincent had not yet studied drawing formally but his sketches were invested with such a personal style that he was able to communicate perfectly the things that were around him and the way he saw them. Still refusing to change his mind about what he wanted to do with his life, Vincent returned to London. He found employment as a tutor in French and German first at a small school in Kent and then in a poor neighbourhood in London. Contact with others was what interested him, not the work itself. In fact, because his knowledge of languages left much to be desired, Vincent was not very good at his job.

It was the minor part of his work which he liked most. Vincent was given the job of collecting students' fees, and as he visited their families, he became familiar with the miserable conditions of London's East End. The life of a worker in the most industrialized nation in the world at the end of the nineteenth century was hard. Vincent's exposure to it in London made a strong impression on him and reinforced his desire to work with the poor and the humble. He became an assistant to a Methodist minister, the Reverend Mr. Jones, and began to preach. In his sermons, he preached that man was a stranger on earth and his life a voyage fraught with storms. Although his English was poor, he spoke dramatically and his sincerity rang out in his words. If he was effective, it was because he believed so strongly in what he was saying. But in reality, it was Vincent who was the stranger in a strange land. Instead of giving comfort to his listeners, his words often troubled them.

Vincent was going through a deep spiritual crisis as he tried to find some sort of balance in his life. He returned to Holland for Christmas 1878 and spent it with his parents in Atten, near Zundert. As a result of this visit, his family decided to help him in his ambition to become a minister. They helped him establish himself in Amsterdam so he could begin theological studies, after which, if he wanted to continue, he could follow in the footsteps of his father and grandfather.

But in Amsterdam, Vincent suffered a new setback: he failed his entrance exams. Instead of giving up, however, he decided that he would study on his own. He went to a centre near Brussels in Laeken to train to become a lay preacher and three months later, in November 1878, he moved to the Borinage, the Belgian coal-mining district and began to share the lives of the miners. The drawings he enclosed with his letters during this period multiplied as he portrayed the life of the people among whom he lived. But his father, concerned about the life his son was leading — sleeping on a pallet on the floor, caring for the incurably ill, and deprived of all comforts — went in search of him and brought him home.

Living once more with his family, Vincent began to take up drawing seriously. With pencil and paper in hand, he released his pent-up feelings for the poor and miserable in his drawings. Painting became his new "religion".

It was during this period that Vincent went to Courrières, a mining district in northern France. He intended to visit the painter Jules Breton who lived and worked there, expressing his social concerns in his canvases. But Vincent never met him: when he saw the elegant studio where Breton worked, he fled, disillusioned.

Nevertheless, he took back to Belgium strong memories of the transparent and limpid French skies and nurtured them in his soul. Setting himself up next in Brussels, he began to study drawing systematically. Theo watched over him from a distance and helped him out financially. It was on Theo's advice that Vincent began lessons with a young painter, Anthon von Rappard, a student at the Academy. Vincent learned the laws of perspective from him. A friendship soon developed between them and Vincent spent many happy hours in Von Rappard's studio. Those that he spent in his hotel room near the station were less satisfying. He spent the time drawing endlessly, learning to draw the human body, trying to apply what he was learning from anatomy books on the figures he had sketched when he was in London and Borinage.

It was a calmer Vincent that Theo and his parents found when he visited them in Etten in April 1881. He received a warm welcome from them and then went on to rediscover the countryside of his childhood which he could now draw. The farms, fields, forests, mills, and carts, the farming implements, the shoemaker, the blacksmith, all no longer held secrets for Vincent. Fresh from his studies in Brussels, he could render on paper a methodical and sensitive inventory of what he saw.

Vincent's cousin, Mauve, also an artist advised Vincent when he visited him in The Hague to draw from nature, so, working in pencil, pen, charcoal, India ink, and watercolours, he drew his parents and his sister Wilhelmine as well as the peasants going about their work. The figures have hard brusque contours and reflect their fatigue. Only in his watercolours are these realistic figures softened somewhat.

During this very fertile period he once again fell in love, also with disastrous consequences. This time the object of his affections was his young cousin, Kee Vos, a widow whom he knew through his parents. She chose to remain faithful to the memory of her dead husband rather than accept Vincent's proposal.

Vincent's feelings were so strong, however, that he put them to a literal test of fire. Vincent had gone to Amsterdam to call on Kee's parents to ask them to let him see Kee, who had gone there to get away from Vincent. To show how determined he was in his love for her, he held his hand over a burning oil lamp. It proved to be in vain; the scars on his heart lasted longer than the scars on his hand.

He then set himself up on the outskirts of The Hague and began to paint street scenes and gardens with great detail, trying to capture the atmosphere of the place in the tradition of the old Dutch masters. Here his old love for engraving came to his aid. He covered the walls of his room with reproductions of his favourites.

In January 1882, Vincent met another woman in the streets of his neighbourhood in The Hague. He immediately engulfed her with his overwhelming need for love and self-sacrifice. Christine Sien was a prostitute. Vincent took her in, along with her baby (and another child on the way) and made her his companion and model. His most famous portrait he drew is called *Sorrow*. She is portrayed sitting, hunched over, with her elbows on her knees. Although her face is hidden, her nude body, drawn with no attempt to romanticize or beautify it, reveals the drama of her life. But in spite of his efforts, Vincent's relationship with Christine did not last long. After giving birth to the second child, she began to drink again and Vincent was unable to help her. When he decided to move to the country, Christine did not go with him.

The wild region of Drenthe where Vincent went seduced him so completely that he wrote, "if I cannot stay here forever, I would prefer never to have seen it." But while nature was generous and inspired him with ideas, the local country folk were inhospitable and suspicious. Vincent was not able to make friends with them as he had hoped. Penniless and alone, he returned home.

In December 1883 we find him in Neunen where his father had a new parish. By now, relations with his family had become strained. Feeling misunderstood, Vincent once more decided to leave the family home and rented two rooms nearby. One of them became the first studio he had ever had, for even while he had lived with his parents he had had to paint in the wash-house. It was in this studio in Neunen rented from M. Shafrath, the Catholic sacristan, in 1885, that Vincent van Gogh, the son and grandson of Protestant ministers, painted one of his most famous works, *The Potato Eaters*.

It was no haphazard creation. Van Gogh had been studying the human body for a long time and had given much thought to the colours of his palette. The Impressionists with their brilliant and free brushstrokes were fashionable at the time, but Vincent was searching for his own style, one that would best express what he felt. In a nearby village, an old goldsmith had asked him to decorate his dining room with religious compositions. Vincent proposed doing six rural scenes showing a series of workers in the fields, to be painted in colours to harmonize with the wood tones in the room. Bistre and bituminous browns appeared in his palette with whites and fragmented tones giving a luminous quality to his darker values. He captured figures in characteristic poses as in the *Peasant Woman Sweeping*, and did endless studies of hands and faces, drawing a group of fifty heads with remarkable force.

For still-lifes such as *Still-life with Five Bottles and Cup*, he was inspired by simple-shaped bottles, pitchers and cups of common usage rather than by fine objects. So it was that by the time he painted *The Potato Eaters*, he had found his own style.

A year later, Van Gogh moved again, this time to France. Perhaps it was his father's death or perhaps it was a desire to be close to his brother who had moved to Paris that led him to pack up his belongings once more. In any case, when he left Holland this time, it was for good; he was never to return.

Before he went to Paris, however, Vincent stopped in Antwerp for a few months. Rubens paintings were scattered throughout the city in churches and museum. These works affected Vincent profoundly, and he visited and revisited these places frequently to view the paintings. Here, he painted his first self-portrait.

Van Gogh spent the next two years, from 1886 to 1888, in Paris. They were fruitful years. Exposed to Impressionist painting, Vincent developed his own way of using the strong colours he loved so well. He became friendly with Deural, Signac, Anquetin, Bernard and other young painters who were drawn to the Impressionist movement and wanted to revive it. He formed ties with Toulouse-Lautrec, admired Pissarro and was captivated by Gauguin.

"The French air clears the brain and does one good — a world of good," he wrote. Vincent lived with his brother, who managed a gallery in Montmartre, and continued to study drawing. He copied plaster casts and worked with live models in the studio of the painter Cormon and he began to paint flowers. "I have painted... red poppies, blue cornflowers, lilies of the valley, red and white roses, and yellow chrysanthemums," he wrote in a letter, "looking for contrasts of blue with orange, red with green, yellow with violet..." The result of these experiments is his painting *Wild Flowers in a Vase*. But life was not all roses even in those happy days. Alternating between

periods of elation and great bursts of anger, Vincent's was a difficult nature, passionate and obstinate. Even Theo at times found him difficult to get along with. "It's as if he were two people," confided Theo to his sister. "It's sad; he really is his own worst enemy."

By now, the two brothers had left their small apartment on the Rue de Laval (today the Rue Victor-Mercier) and moved into a large house near Montmartre. The windows looked out over the rooftops of Paris. Now besides painting lively coloured flowers, Vincent began to paint new scenes — gardens and windmills — which reminded him of his childhood (he did three of the Moulin de la Galette alone), and street scenes of Paris and its outskirts, such as *Corner of Voyer-d'Argenson Park at Asnières* and *Bathing Place on the Seine at Asnières*. These lively subjects called for a lighter palette.

He had animated discussions with other artists in cafés and cabarets. These experiences inspired paintings like *Interior of a Restaurant* and *Woman Sitting in the Café du Tambourin*, and reflected his friendship with Toulouse-Lautrec. Another important painting from this period was a *Portrait of Père Tanguy*, an art supplies dealer and a friend to many struggling painters. In exchange for paints and materials, Tanguy often accepted paintings from his customers, who at the time could find no other buyer for their works. These same paintings would one day hang in the greatest museums in the world. Van Gogh's second *Self-Portrait* came right after his *Portrait of Père Tanguy*. Both reflect Van Gogh's desire to express character, above all, in his portraits.

The two years he spent in Paris were rich in conversation and friendship and were a great help in the development of his style. They were happy years for Van Gogh and paved the road for him on the way to becoming a great painter. But commercial success still eluded him. After two years in Paris, he paid a visit to his friend Emile Bernard at Asnières. It was a significant visit for it gave him a taste for the French countryside. He was already beginning to tire of Paris and he decided he wanted a change. And so, leaving his brother in Paris, he set off for Provence. Though he had never been there before, he imagined it as a kind of paradise.

When he arrived in the Midi, in February 1888, it was blanketed in snow. As the snow melted, the new blossoms on the tree looked to Van Gogh like clumps of snow that had lingered on into the spring. This scene became the subject of several paintings, influenced to some extent by the newly-discovered Japanese prints that were all the rage in Paris.

He settled in Arles, and he dreamed of establishing in this little village with its clear skies, a place where artists could come to live and work. It was a dream he had had for a long time. Meanwhile, he worked night and day, drawing inspiration from the countryside of Provence around him, and was constantly "fed by nature." In his painting *The Langlois Bridge* the crystalline light of Arles shines through. The sun-filled countryside of the Midi where the wheat seems more yellow than anywhere else in the world becomes the subject of many paintings, including *The Plain at la Crau*. In one sitting one evening during the mistral, Van Gogh painted *Summer Evening*. He reinterpreted a painting by his Parisian friend Emile Bernard, *Breton Women in a Meadow*. Inspired by another painting of a great master whom he admired, he painted his own version, *The Sower*. He went as far as Saintes-Maries-de-la-Mer where he painted the little farm houses (*Farmhouses at Saintes-Maries*) and the boats (*Boats on the Beach at Saintes-Maries*).

Nights in Provence, both indoors and outdoors, held special meanings and colours for Van Gogh. Anyone who had seen Vincent wearing his strange hat with lighted candles attached to it, seated at his easel along the Rhône to paint *The Starry Night* would have shaken his head and wondered if it was worth all that fuss. Today, as we look at the unforgettable nightscapes that only Van Gogh could paint, of course we would say yes, it was worth it.

The colours he was then using were violent and bold ("certainly, time will not soften them," he wrote to his brother). In *The Night Café*, yellow, dominant in many of his compositions, reigns. It is the same in *Still-Life with Onions and Drawing Board*. For *Van Gogh's Bedroom in Arles* he also used strong colours. He wrote of this in a letter to his friend Gauguin. "It has amused me a great deal to do this little interior scene, so unimportant in itself... with flat tones, but stroked on broadly, with a full brush, the pale lilac walls, the floor a broken and faded red, the chairs and bed in chrome yellow, the pillow and sheets a pale lemon green, the spread blood red, the toilet table orange, the basin blue and the window green. What I want to get across is a feeling of absolute rest through all these different colours, with no white save the one small note of the mirror in its black frame." Vincent also painted *Van Gogh's Chair and Pipe* during the same period.

He also continued to paint portraits. "I want to do figures, figures and more figures," he wrote to Theo. From this period comes *La Mousmé* and *Woman Reading a Novel*. Vincent often had difficulty getting models for they were expensive. In fact, he sometimes had to beg them to work for him — they had no idea what he was doing. His friend Joseph Roulin, a postman in Arles, came to his aid and posed for him (*The Postman Joseph Roulin*) as well as other members of the Roulin family — his brother Armand (*Portrait of Armand Roulin*) and Madame Augustine who appears in Van Gogh's work *La Berceuse*.

Next, Van Gogh began his *Sunflowers* series. While working on these flowers, he became obsessed with the colour yellow, exploring every aspect of it. During this period, Gauguin came down to join him. Ironically it was the arrival of his dearest friend, a painter whom Van Gogh considered a master, that provoked his first nervous breakdown and threatened his mental stability. The two artists lived together and it was through their intense day-to-day contact that Van Gogh began to realize that the two men had very different principles and ways of looking at painting. The style that Van Gogh used to reinterpret *Les Alyscamps*, inspired by his friend, demonstrates this. Shortly after, when Gauguin painted a portrait of him, Van Gogh refused to accept it. He did not want to recognize himself in Gauguin's portrait of a man painting sunflowers with an air of madness. After a violent argument, which drove Gauguin back to Paris, Vincent cut off his own ear with a razor. He documented this in another self-portrait, *Self-Portrait with Bandaged Ear*.

At the Saint-Paul hospital where he was taken after this episode, he was attended by a young man, Dr. Rey, who became one of his greatest admirers. Once he had recovered Vincent painted a portrait of the doctor. But morally and psychologically, the wounds of his breakdown were far from being mended. Theo was about to be married and Vincent saw this as a kind of abandonment. So finally, with Dr. Rey's support, he agreed to move to the hospital in Saint-Rémy-de-Provence, with the hope of recovering his health there. On this sad note, his stay in Arles ended. During the one short year that he spent there he had produced around two hundred paintings and one hundred drawings.

Van Gogh accepted his new situation with resignation. We can guess what was going on inside him from his new self-portrait. Painting was his comfort. In *The Prisoners' Walk*, he portrays the faces of his new companions and it is likely that he has included himself among them. In his other paintings of the hospital, he represses his dramatic experience there by depicting views of the hospital gardens transformed by his imagination so that they seem like quiet corners painted during a pleasant holiday.

But the crises returned and drove Van Gogh to despair. While he was suffering one of his attacks, he would stop painting, but as soon as he felt better, he would return to his work. He produced one hundred and fifty paintings and one hundred drawings. Yet his art had changed. Colour was no longer the most important aspect; form took over, and it was of a kind that was undulating and upsetting. He painted cypresses as if they were flames (*The Cypresses*, *Wheatfield with Cypresses*, *Cypresses, with Two Women in the Foreground*, *Road with Cypress and Star*), turbulent skies, and decorticated olive trees baring their souls. He invented this tumultuous nature from his room where he was kept confined most of the time. There he also painted *L'Arlésienne* which was inspired by a drawing by Gauguin whom he continued to admire in spite of the rupture in their friendship.

Thanks to his stay in Saint-Rémy, Vincent was not long in recovering his health. In May 1890 he travelled to Paris where he visited his brother Theo, now married and the father of a son. His acceptance as an artist was confirmed when he was mentioned in a revue in "Mercure de France". With pleasure he saw again his old friends, Père Tanguy, Pissarro and Toulouse-Lautrec. He rediscovered the canvases he had painted earlier in Paris and Provence that his brother had kept and he felt pleased with his progress. But this was to be only a brief visit. City life tired and overstimulated him; he stayed in Paris only four days.

By now his wanderings were motivated by a need to avoid another attack of his illness. This time he travelled to Auvers-sur-Oise to rest. There he met a Dr. Gachet who was also a painter, with a soul as troubled as his own. Dr. Gachet believed that painting was the best therapy for Vincent and we find the doctor's troubled face revealed shortly thereafter (*Portrait of Dr. Gachet*). *Chestnut Blossoms* and *Vase with Carnations and Gillyflowers* were two paintings of flowers done during that period. They are very different from those of his Parisian period. The yellows and bright colours have disappeared. In their place are warm but softer colours. In *Thatched Cottages at Cordeville* we catch a glimpse of the rolling countryside of Auvers that surrounded Van Gogh.

Once, Theo came to visit him, bringing his wife and infant son who was named after Vincent. During their stay, Vincent made a gift to his nephew of a bird's nest that he had found when he was a boy; he had kept it throughout the years as a kind of talisman. At one point Vincent revealed to his brother his dream of a future life they would share and Theo seemed to approve of the idea. They would have a house in the country and all live together. But alas these were only dreams. Theo was having financial difficulties and his own health was precarious. The money he had once sent to Vincent regularly began to be delayed. Once more Vincent felt abandoned. It was during this period that his dramatic work *Crows in the Wheatfield* was painted.

When his brother failed to visit him again, Vincent decided to go to Paris himself. The meeting of Theo, his wife and Vincent on a Sunday at the beginning of July, ended in a lively discussion in which Theo revealed that he was thinking of going back to Holland. Things seemed to be falling apart around Vincent. There seemed to be nowhere to turn. Even his friend Dr. Gachet was away on business. Vincent ended up spending July 14th, Bastille Day, completely alone. In a letter to Theo written on July 23rd, he spoke of the uselessness of life and on July 27th, a Sunday, he headed for the wheatfields as he had done so many times before. But this time he took with him not his paintbrushes or easel, but only a pistol for shooting at crows. In a moment of profound despair he turned it upon himself. Wounded, he managed to drag himself back to the Café Ravoux where he lived and Dr. Gachet was called in. Upon examining him, he said the bullet could not be removed. When Theo arrived the next morning, he found his brother lying peacefully in bed, smoking his pipe. The two brothers spent the whole day together, speaking Dutch and finding once more the harmony of old times. That evening Theo refused to leave and spent the night lying next to his brother in the same bed. Vincent died in the early hours of the morning, around 1:30 a.m. on July 28th, 1890.

In a letter he had written to his brother not long before, he said: "I do not need to go out of my way to express sadness and the extremity of loneliness." In another letter he had written "Do you know what I often think of? About what I already said to you sometime ago... that even if I did not succeed, I still believed that what I have worked at will be carried on. Not directly perhaps, but one is not alone in believing things are true."

Hope and despair — twin poles of the same life.

1. Peasant Woman Sweeping - 1885. Kröller-Müller Stichting Museum, Otterlo - *In 1884-85 Van Gogh went through one of his most intense and fertile periods of development in terms of expression in his paintings. He portrayed peasants in a wide variety of poses reflecting the humble world of village craftsmen as well as painting many still-lifes.*

2. Still-Life with Five Bottles and Cup - 1884-85. Kröller-Müller Stichting Museum, Otterlo - *This painting was done when Van Gogh was in Neunen, a period when he was seeking to express the essence of objects in a simple manner. He painted the modest everyday objects of the peasants' world as symbols of the most sacred values of life.*

3. The Potato Eaters (detail) - 1885. Vincent van Gogh Museum, Amsterdam - *This version, the third of that name, was painted in May 1885. It marks the end of his formal studies and the end of his interest in chiaroscuro and the use of heavy strokes- techniques he perfected while he was in Neunen. In this composition he expresses his love for the land and the workers.*

4. Bathing Place on the Seine at Asnières - 1887. Mr. & Mrs. Paul Mellon Collection, Upperville - *This painting, done during the summer of 1887 after he had been in Paris for a year, shows the enormous influence Parisian culture had on Van Gogh. The lesson of the Impressionists, to whom he was closely tied, is evident.*

5. The Moulin de la Galette - 1886. Kröller-Müller Stichting Museum, Otterlo - *While Van Gogh worked on this painting of Montmartre he was in daily contact with Impressionist, Divisionist, and Synthesist friends, but their concepts did not influence his own instinctive way of expressing emotion. The vigour and density of his brushstrokes are in fact quite different from the predominant styles of the period.*

6. The Moulin de la Galette - 1886-87. Museo Nacional de Bellas Artes, Buenos Aires - *Montmartre was Van Gogh's favourite part of Paris, with its windmills reminding him of those of his childhood. He painted several versions of this windmill, discussing and comparing it to those of his friends Lautrec and Signac.*

7. The Moulin de la Galette - 1887. Museum of Art, Carnegie Institute, Pittsburgh - *When van Gogh worked on this canvas in March 1887, he had already met Gauguin and Seurat. He examined their studies of Synthesism and Divisionism and adapted what interested him to his own needs. His brushstrokes are often elongated but they are not exaggerated, nor does colour become symbolically abstract.*

8. The Plain of La Crau - 1888. Vincent van Gogh Museum, Amsterdam - *At Arles, after his experiences in Paris, Van Gogh worked on perfecting his use of luminous colour and learned to construct an image with a single stroke. During the summer of 1888, he painted the countryside of Provence, a landscape that stimulated his creative fantasy, showing it in bright sunlight.*

9. Summer Evening - 1888. Kunstmuseum, Winterthur - *Summer brought about an explosion of colour in Van Gogh's work. He discovered the Mediterranean countryside with its ripening wheatfields in shades of the blues and yellows he found so seductive. In this painting, made at the end of June, he intentionally used intense colours declaring that "the night is richer in colour than the day."*

10. Corner of Voyer-d'Argenson Park at Asnières - 1887. Private collection - *In the summer of 1887 Van Gogh was able to explore the French countryside. He visited the neighbouring villages around Paris, taking copious notes. Even though he was usually alone in his ramblings, he was in contact with other artists such as Seurat, Signac and Bernard.*

11. Interior of a Restaurant - Kröller-Müller Stichting Museum, Otterlo - *A new experience, a new technique or a new theory was always an occasion for Van Gogh to enrich his palette and develop his artistic abilities further, but he never gave up his originality which was free of any pre-established ways. The Pointillist technique he uses here shows his constant search for expressive synthesis.*

12. Woman Sitting in the Café du Tambourin - 1887. Vincent van Gogh Museum, Amsterdam - *Toulouse-Lautrec, in a painting similar to this, portrayed the same woman in the same pose. The two painters, whose backgrounds and artistic temperaments were so different, showed similar sensitivity in their treatment of the subject.*

13. Portrait of Père Tanguy - 1887. Stavros S. Niarchos Collection, Athens - *This modest seller of artists' supplies, a friend and admirer of Van Gogh, was portrayed by many artists. Van Gogh's version, done at the end of 1887, serves as an introduction to his Arles period, shown by the quality of his brushstrokes as well as the intensity of his colours.*

14. Self-Portrait - 1887. Vincent van Gogh Museum, Amsterdam - *Van Gogh took divisionist techniques and made them his own in this self-portrait painted in 1887. He attempted to intensify the expression of the face with short strokes and the use of colour. The brushstrokes radiate from the face as if emanating from some luminous source.*

15. Les Alyscamps - 1888. Kröller-Müller Stichting Museum, Otterlo - *Obsessed with the expressive value of colour, Van Gogh admired painters who constructed space by using bold arbitrary colours. Gauguin's revolutionary chromatic example predominates in this painting.*

16. The Langlois Bridge - 1888. Wallraf-Richartz Museum, Cologne - *The little drawbridge, possibly the last version in a series, is painted in the Japanese style with light, flat colours, capturing an emotional intensity that foretells the works to come that summer.*

17. Boats on the Beach at Saintes-Maries - 1888. Vincent van Gogh Museum, Amsterdam - *The unreal accent which Van Gogh gives to reality vibrates in this marvellous painting, radiating abstract colours, done in the summer of 1888.*

18. Breton Women in a Meadow - 1888. Galleria d'Arte Moderna, Grassi Collection, Milan - *Van Gogh continuously studied the old masters as well as his contemporaries, assimilating their innovations and discoveries. This painting from 1888 is an original interpretation of a work by Emile Bernard, transformed by Van Gogh with great expressive liberty.*

19. Sunflowers - 1887. The Metropolitan Museum of Art, Rogers Fund 1949, New York - *Sunflowers were an important subject for Van Gogh who used them as a vehicle to experiment with deep blue and yellow. However, the yellow, a colour that would appear often, no longer explodes with the same sunny intensity that it did under the skies of the south of France.*

20. Wild Flowers in a Vase - Private collection, USA - *The date of this painting is uncertain but the clear chromatic work, the study of different colour tones, and their juxtaposition on the canvas suggest that it was painted in 1888, which corresponds to the growing maturity and artistic evolution of Van Gogh in that year.*

21. The Café Terrace on the Place du Forum, Arles, at Night - 1888. Kröller-Müller Stichting Museum, Otterlo - *Alongside the stars shining like a far-off refuge, the disquieting light from the café draws one in with a menacing seduction. The painting is direct and immediate, revealing a symbolic concept that gives it meaning. Painted in 1888, it is one of Van Gogh's most important works.*

22. Van Gogh's Chair and Pipe - 1888. Tate Gallery, London - *Arles was undisputedly the most important period in Van Gogh's artistic development and he painted most of his major works there. This canvas, painted in December 1888, shows how even the simplest objects can be given meaning through the use of colour.*

23. The Night Café - 1888. Yale University Art Gallery, bequest of Stephen Carlton Clark, New Haven - *Van Gogh wrote: "I have tried to show that the café is a place where a man can ruin himself, go mad, commit a crime... I have tried to express the terrible passions of humanity through red and green." The work is dated September 1888.*

24. Van Gogh's Bedroom in Arles - 1888. Vincent van Gogh Museum, Amsterdam - *As in the two versions of the "Night Café", the intimate and luminous harmony of this painting, done in the same period, gives a feeling of tranquillity and rest, through the use of contrasting colours and accents.*

25. La Mousmé - 1888. National Gallery of Art, Chester Dale Collection, Washington - *Using luminous tones, Van Gogh painted a delicate and typical image, interpreting in his own way the Japanese prints in vogue at the time. With their characteristic use of colour zones, they had a profound influence on him.*

26. Woman Reading a Novel - 1888. Private collection, England - *Painted in November 1888, this canvas shows how Van Gogh painted the most ordinary subjects with an understanding of their inherent value, using specific colours to get beyond the simple appearance of things.*

27. Portrait of Armand Roulin - 1888. Folkwang Museum, Essen - *This portrait, painted while Gauguin was in Arles in November 1888, highlights Van Gogh's capacity to choose tones of poetic serenity to express his deep human understanding of those he cared for. The Roulin family were among the few people with whom he had a strong friendship.*

28. Still-Life with Onions and Drawing Board - 1889. Kröller-Müller Stichting Museum, Otterlo - *Van Gogh's originality lies not only in his expressive use of colour - which became a kind of personal language - but also in certain ideas he had about composition. In this painting from January 1889, the subject seen from an angle is much more alive than it would have been if seen from the front.*

29. Vase with Sunflowers - 1889. Vincent van Gogh Museum, Amsterdam - *With his "Sunflower" series, the artist decorated the interior of the little yellow house he rented in Arles. In this canvas of January 1889, the exaltation of colour reaches an almost hallucinatory intensity. He has achieved this by using one dominant tone, varying only its luminosity.*

30. The Postman Joseph Roulin - 1889. Kröller-Müller Stichting Museum, Otterlo - *This work was painted at the height of Van Gogh's experiments with luminosity. His dramatic break with Gauguin was a terrible shock but as he himself later wrote, his ability to paint "was not even scratched". His expressive powers are intact in this portrait of his friend Roulin.*

31. La Berceuse (Portrait of Madame Augustine Roulin) - 1889. Private collection, USA - *After the dramatic days around Christmas 1888 and his break with Gauguin, only the Roulin family remained to receive his attentions and friendship. In January 1889 he did several portraits of Madame Augustine Roulin; this one reveals his mastery of colour.*

32. Wheatfield with Cypresses - 1889. National Gallery, London - *The artistic and spiritual evolution of the painter in Saint-Rémy made him aware of the basic rhythms of nature playing around him. In this painting of 1888, the undulating lines of each element of the countryside mirror the tumult of the painter's own life.*

33. The Cypresses - 1889. The Metropolitan Museum of Art, Rogers Fund 1949, New York - *This painting dates to the beginning of Van Gogh's stay at the hospital in Saint-Rémy around June 1889. The artist expresses his emotional tension in his use of colour as well as in the convulsive rhythm of his brushstrokes, which seem to shake the cypresses and make the skies tremble.*

34. L'Arlésienne (Portrait of Madame Ginoux) - 1890. Kröller-Müller Stichting Museum, Otterlo - *It is interesting to compare the two portraits of Madame Ginoux. The first, painted in Arles in 1888, is characterized by an explosion of intense colour. In the second, painted in Saint-Rémy at the beginning of 1890 and inspired by a drawing by Gauguin, the colours are more subdued. The painting's focus is on the expression of the face.*

35. Self-Portrait with Bandaged Ear - 1889. Courtauld Institute Galleries, London - *Van Gogh painted this work shortly after the dramatic episode with Gauguin which ended their friendship. Yet, in this painting, as in his other famous "Self-portrait with Cut Ear and Pipe", he depicts himself as strangely serene, almost indifferent.*

36. Road with Cypress and Star - 1890. Kröller-Müller Stichting Museum, Otterlo - *In this nocturnal landscape of May 1890, we find a unity of inspiration with the other works finished during his stay in Saint-Rémy that Van Gogh had not hitherto achieved. Details are played down to bring out the whirling rhythms that envelop the painting.*

37. Cypresses, with two Women in the Foreground - 1889. Kröller-Müller Stichting Museum, Otterlo - *Van Gogh celebrated his intense desire to fuse with nature with an explosion of colour. In this painting, done when he was going through a difficult emotional period, the somber colours of the cypresses resemble enormous flames that reflect his own inner turmoil.*

38. Farm Houses at Saintes-Maries - 1888. Private collection, USA - *In the bright atmosphere of the south of France, Van Gogh's colours became pure and intense and his drawings more simplified. Under the skies of Provence, a natural mirror of his immense and deep spiritual desires, he seemed to create a harmonious fusion with nature and the countryside.*

39. Chestnut Blossoms - 1890. Stiftung Sammlung E.G. Bührle, Zürich - *This was one of the first paintings Van Gogh did in Auvers. He was still fascinated by nature and his accomplishment in composition continued to mature. But knowing the importance that each colour held for him, one can sense the tragic depths of his feelings.*

40. Thatched Cottages at Cordeville - 1890. Musée du Louvre, Paris - *The end of his stay in Auvers-sur-Oise, from May 1890 onward, was very agitated, as one can see in this painting in which a whirlwind seems to be shaking up everything, reflecting the artist's own torment.*

41. Portrait of Dr. Gachet - 1890. Musée d'Orsay, Paris - *"I would love to paint portraits,"* wrote Van Gogh, *"which in a hundred years will seem like ghosts to those who see them."* Gachet's fatigue leaps out of the deep blue background of this portrait of Van Gogh's friend, painted a few months before Vincent's death.

42. Self-Portrait - 1890. Musée d'Orsay, Paris - *In this self-portrait executed in Saint-Rémy during his worst period, Van Gogh expresses the change he has undergone, with the dull tones of his solitude replacing the intense sunny colours of his previous pictures.*

43. Vase with Carnations and Gillyflowers - 1890. Private collection, USA - *When Van Gogh painted his bedroom, he wrote to his brother Theo that the predominant yellow colour was meant to suggest a sense of repose. In this painting, yellow has disappeared and is replaced by cool tones.*

44. Crows in the Wheatfields - 1890. Vincent van Gogh Museum, Amsterdam - *During his stay in Auvers, Van Gogh went from painting landscapes that expressed his desire for inner peace to paintings that bespoke a fury out of control. This dramatic work, painted some twenty days before his death, seems to be an agonized cry.*

1. *Peasant Woman Sweeping* - 1885. Kröller-Müller Stichting Museum,
Otterlo

2. *Still-Life with Five Bottles and Cup* - 1884-85. Kröller- Müller Stichting Museum, Otterlo

3. *The Potato Eaters* (detail) - 1885. Vincent van Gogh
Museum, Amsterdam

4. *Bathing Place on the Seine at Asnières* - 1887. Mr & Mrs Paul Mellon Collection, Upperville

5. *The Moulin de la Galette* - 1886. Kröller-Müller Stichting Museum, Otterlo

6. *The Moulin de la Galette* - 1986-87. Museo Nacional de Bellas Artes, Buenos Aires

7. *The Moulin de la Galette* - 1887. Museum of Art, Carnegie Institute, Pittsburgh

8. *The Plain of la Crau* - 1888. Vincent van Gogh Museum, Amsterdam

9. *Summer Evening* - 1888. Kunstmuseum, Winterthur

10. *Corner of Voyer-d'Argenson Park at Asnières* - 1887. Private collection

11. *Interior of a Restaurant*. Kröller-Müller Stichting Museum, Otterlo

12. *Woman Sitting in the Café du Tambourin* - 1887. Vincent van Gogh Museum, Amsterdam

14. *Self-Portrait* - 1887. Vincent van Gogh Museum, Amsterdam

15. *Les Alyscamps* - 1888. Kröller-Müller Stichting Museum, Otterlo

16. *The Langlois Bridge* - 1888. Wallraf-Richartz Museum, Cologne

17. *Boats on the Beach at Saintes-Maries* - 1888. Vincent van Gogh Museum, Amsterdam

18. *Breton Women in a Meadow* - 1888. Galleria d'Arte Moderna, Grassi Collection, Milan

19. *Sunflowers* - 1887. The Metropolitan Museum of Art,
Rogers Fund 1949, New York

20. *Wild Flowers in a Vase*. Private collection, USA

22. *Van Gogh's Chair and Pipe* - 1888. Tate Gallery, London

23. *The Night Café* - 1888. Yale University Art Gallery, bequest
of Stephen Carlton Clark, New Haven

24. *Van Gogh's Bedroom in Arles* - 1888. Vincent van Gogh Museum, Amsterdam

25. *La Mousmé* - 1888. National Gallery of Art, Chester Dale Collection, Washington

26. *Woman Reading a Novel* - 1888. Private collection, England

27. *Portrait of Armand Roulin* - 1888. Folkwang Museum, Essen

30. *The Postman Joseph Roulin* - 1889. Kröller-Müller Stichting Museum, Otterlo

31. *La Berceuse (Portrait of Madame Augustine Roulin)* - 1889. Private collection, USA

34. *L'Arlésienne (Portrait of Madame Ginoux)* - 1890. Kröller-Müller
Stichting Museum, Otterlo

35. *Self-Portrait with Bandaged Ear* - 1889. Courtauld Institute Galleries, London

36. *Road with Cypress and Star* - 1890. Kröller-Müller Stichting Museum, Otterlo

37. *Cypresses, with two Women in the Foreground* - 1889. Kröller-Müller Stichting Museum, Otterlo

38. *Farm Houses at Saintes-Maries* - 1888. Private collection, USA

39. *Chestnut Blossoms* - 1890. Stiftung Sammlung E.G. Bührle, Zürich

40. *Thatched Cottages at Cordeville* - 1890. Musée du Louvre, Paris

42. *Self-Portrait* - 1890. Musée d'Orsay, Paris

43. *Vase with Carnations and Gillyflowers* - 1890. Private collection, USA

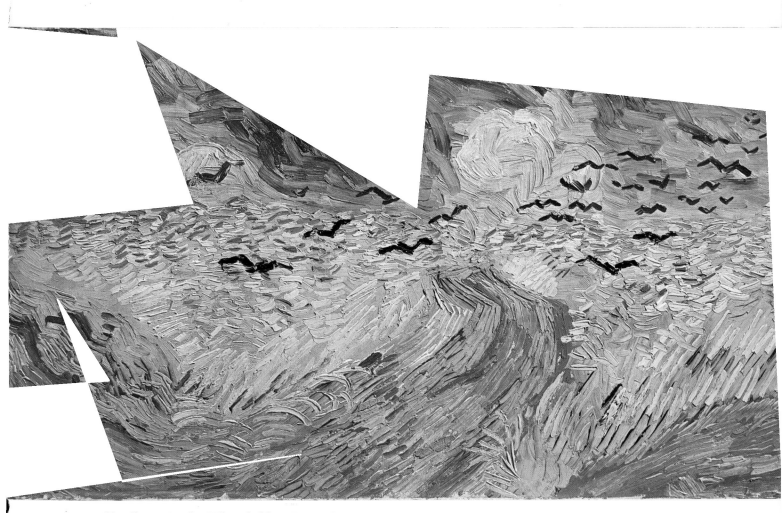

44. *Crows in the Wheatfield* - 1890. Vincent van Gogh Museum, Amsterdam

Editor in chief Anna Maria Mascheroni

Art director Luciano Raimondi

Text Alberta Melanotte

Translation Kerry Milis

Production Art, Bologna

Photo Credits Gruppo Editoriale Fabbri S.p.A., Milan
Copyright © 1988 by Gruppo Editoriale S.p.A., Milan
Published by Park Lane
An imprint of Books & Toys Limited
The Grange
Grange Yard
LONDON
SE1 3AG

ISBN 1-85627-180-3

This edition published 1991

Printed in Italy by Gruppo Editoriale Fabbri S.p.A., Milan